An Illustrated History of American
CUSTOM
MOTORCYCLES

An Illustrated History of American
CUSTOM
MOTORCYCLES

ANDREW MORLAND & PETER HENSHAW

OSPREY
AUTOMOTIVE

ACKNOWLEDGEMENTS

As with any book, this one would never have been completed without the help of a great many people. First, there were all those owners who patiently waited while Andrew Morland took pictures of their amazing custom motorcycles – Brian Bussaglia, Chris Le Sauvage Jr, Ronald Torbich, Rusty Wright, Tommy Jansson, Ken Denison, Steve Myers, Tina Holtman, Gary Saxton, Ken Goldsbury, Tom Fedorowski and Jim Randolph.

Of the professional customizers, thanks go to Battistini's, Donnie Smith, Mallard Teal and Dave Perewitz (of Cycle Fab). The extract on page 55 is reproduced with the permission of Simon & Schuster, London, and is taken from *Hog Fever* by Richard La Plante. © Richard La Plante, 1994.

All photographs by Andrew Morland, except pages 13, 14 and 28, all taken from Mike Clay's *Café Racers* (Osprey 1988), a gem which the publishers intend to reprint in the near future. The Indian bobber on page 15 was photographed by Garry Stuart, and the "Captain America" replica on page 40 by Roland Brown.

The quote from Michael Diamond on page 46 comes with the permission of the Birmingham Museum & Art Gallery. Finally, thanks go to Richard Taylor of Bespoke/Taylor Made (especially for the detailed specifications), to Osprey for taking the project on and as always to everyone we've omitted to mention.

Peter Henshaw, Andrew Morland

First published in Great Britain in 1997 by Osprey, a division of Reed Books, Michelin House, 81 Fulham Road, London SW3 6RB. Auckland, and Melbourne

© Copyright Reed International Books Ltd 1997

Text by Peter Henshaw.
Photographs by Andrew Morland, unless otherwise indicated.

ISBN 1 85532 614 0

Editor: Shaun Barrington
Design: the Black Spot

Printed and bound in China

For a catalogue of all books published by Osprey Automotive please write to: Osprey Marketing, Reed Books, Michelin House, 81 Fulham Road, London, England SW3 6RB

HALF TITLE PAGE **One thing you won't see at Sturgis are full-face helmets; this silver-topped pudding basin and German-style helmet are a more likely sight**

TITLE PAGE **Ken Denison's Razorback; see page 122. Engine is almost stock, with subtle red finning**

CONTENTS

CHAPTER ONE
WHY CUSTOMIZE?

Elvis Presley, if legend has it right, turned revolution into fashion. From the hip wiggling jungle rhythms which horrified middle America to a mass, mainstream, weekend entertainment. It was the same process that demoted Che Guevara from a revolutionary leader into popstar icon, his designer stubbled face gazing heroically out from thousands of student bedroom walls.

In some ways, the same is true of the custom bike. It started off as a means to an end – bikes were modified purely to make them lighter and faster. But the look that

RIGHT **Stretched early '70s chop, typified by long, long forks, coffin tank and Shovelhead engine. Chrome oil tank is typical too**

LEFT With genuine old Springer forks and no front brake, this Panhead chop could have been built 30 years ago, but the picture was taken at a recent Sturgis, on Main Street

resulted became a badge in itself, a rejection of mainstream values. And finally, as more and more people cottoned on and joined in, it became fashion, the thing to do, which inevitably took the sharpness off any rebellious cutting edge.

So it is with the custom bike movement, which has grown from a few rebellious outcasts (the famed 'One Percenters') to a massive movement of people of all ages, sexes and backgrounds. Look at the shelf-fulls of custom magazines, the rude health of custom bike shows and the huge industry supplying aftermarket parts – this is big business. Quite apart from anything else, custom bike builders and riders are older than ever – this is no a longer symbol of rebellious youth.

But neither has it become an anodyne crowd of sheepish fashion followers. There's more variety and original thinking among custom bikes than ever before. Some are following fashion of course, something made easier by the profusion of bolt-on parts on sale. But there are also enough original and different bikes out there to prove that many others are using it as a means of self-expression and creativity, the urge to produce something genuinely different from everyone else's. And that's why there's such variety in the current custom scene. In 1974, Tony Thacker wrote in Bike magazine:

"A custom bike can be anything that deviates from standard – even just changing the 'bars puts you in the custom class. A chopper is just a custom bike gone berserk, with every aspect of its construction altered and distorted in the extreme."

That was twenty years ago, when the chopper really was the be-all and end-all of the custom bike. In fact it says much for

the chopper's domination that it is still the popular image of what a custom bike is – the stretched frame, raked forks, ape-hanger handle bars and stepped seat. Not for nothing did Raleigh, the British bicycle maker, produce its own 'Raleigh Chopper' in 1969, a three-speed pushbike with all the right styling cues, right down to a sissy bar! It went well with flares and platforms, and even now is having something of a revival (an owner's club has been set up) – in metallic purple, it's seen as the ultimate statement of early '70s kitsch. Like the pavement-sweeping flares and wall-mounted flying ducks of the same era, it's part of our new fascination with the '70s – did we really buy stuff like that?

MOVING ON

Custom bikes have moved on since then. At the time, it looked as if a laid-back chop really was the ultimate custom. But pursuing the same look year after year was a stylistic dead end. Each succeeding summer, forks got longer, bars higher and frames ever more stretched. The result was spectacular to look at (and spectacularly difficult to ride) – but it was more of the same rather than anything really new.

For a while, it looked as if the custom bike was about to stagnate and die. But two things saved the custom movement from

disappearing up its own high-rise handle-bars. From the mid-'70s on, new styles did emerge, and with increasing rapidity as the years went by.

Secondly, though this applies more to the U.S. than Europe, Harley-Davidson finally realised that customizing bikes was good business – factory customs like the SuperGlide, Low Rider and Softail were good sellers, as not everyone wants to create their style statement from scratch. For those with just a little more ambition, Harley officially sanctioned the bolt-on business. With a profusion of bolt-on parts to instantly change the look of your motor-cycle, this was Customizing Made Easy.

But that's just one branch of the custom movement. Within the rest of it there are several styles, all with their own character-istics. The trouble is, trying to categorise the custom bike is a fraught process in itself. Customizing isn't an academic disci-pline, with neatly defined trends, and distinct schools of thought. After all, the whole point is to produce something indi-vidual, different from everything else. It's a result of the builder's own efforts and ideas, not built to a blueprint.

That's especially true of the bikes which evolve over time – for some owners, customizing is an on-going process which never ends. He or she will always be thinking of ways to develop the way the bike looks or performs, so it never actually gets 'finished'. Of course, there are also those who have a clear idea of what they want to start with. When it's finished, the bike will invariably get sold on, for another fresh canvas to take its place.

So the end result, whether definitive or evolving, is a true reflection of what the rider wants to achieve. What it isn't so much now is a reflection of his practical skills. In the early days, customizing was simple enough for anyone to do in their own backyard. But now there are so many specialists, who will paint, engrave, tune, weld and polish, that the majority of bikes reflect the talents of lots of different people, though as ever, the overall look is whatever the owner aspires to. (At the risk of sounding a PC note, it's worth mentioning that 'his' and 'he' are used for convenience only – there are plenty of women involved in customizing). And

LEFT **Smooth detailing on the metalflake-finished frame – note flames on the goose-necked steering head**

because customizing is such an individual process, any attempt to define terms is bound to be tentative – some bikes may borrow from several different styles to create something quite unique. Anyway, what follows is a crude general guide.

CHOP – The original postwar custom. Some people use the word 'chop' as a generic term for any radical custom, but the classic version has raked out forks, high bars, big fat rear tyre with a spindly one at the front, and is still the way many think a custom bike should look. It emerged from late 1940s California as a simple means of making heavy Harleys a little more nimble, by chopping bits off them. As it developed, it was a classic case of form following function; then taking over all together. At first, Harley-powered, but just about every British and Japanese engine has been used since.

LOWRIDER – The bike that broke the chop mould. Similar to the chop in its stretched, long wheelbase profile, but the extra length comes more often in the

RIGHT **Low riding Triumphs can be dwarfed by two medium-sized riders. This is a late unit-construction (the engine and gearbox are built as one unit) bike, though the twin discs are later still**

ABOVE **The café racer
essentials are all there:
clip-on bars, rear-set
footrests, racing seat. But
Britain didn't have the
monopoly on the café cult
– this is a German Adler
two-stroke**

frame than forks. The rider sits low (surprise, surprise) clutching pull-back or flat bars. Lowriders had a clear inspiration from drag racing, where bikes were getting ever longer and lower in pursuit of the eight second quarter. Like the chops, they spawned some over-the-top show bikes whose sole aim was to take take things to the extreme.

CAFE RACER – This one developed in Britain and Europe while US riders were busy building chops. The inspiration here is road racing – the rider crouches forward over the polished alloy tank, wrists straining to keep his weight off the clip-on bars, feet on rear-set footrests. Imagine the stance of a jockey, and you're almost there. Most famous incarnations were based on British bikes of the '50s and '60s, often mixing and matching the best engine to the best frame – Triton (Triumph twin in a Norton Featherbed frame) was the most

popular of these. Polished alloy favoured over chrome, though the Americans later made their own adaptation of the style – the cafe – with flat bars and bright colours.

STREET FIGHTER – The cafe racer's natural successor, built by a generation or two down from the ton-up boys who roared up and down English A-roads on Tritons. This look is less subtle, more brutal. It's all about raw power, or at least the impression of power. So everything is styled to make the engine look as big and mean as possible. Seat and tank are small, the bars flat and narrow, with a massive rear tyre to emphasize the muscle. Big Japanese engines, usually fours of 750cc upwards, give the desired presence and tuning potential. Black, either glossy or matt, is a favourite colour scheme. Ever mindful of the market, some of the Japanese factories have tried to produce a ready-made street fighter – the Yamaha V-Max is one of the more spectaculer examples.

RAT – The ratbike is a bit different. The best ones seem to suggest that any attention to aesthetics is a bourgeois superficiality, imposed on the face of motorcycling. In other words, a typical rat has to look completely neglected, cobbled together over the years from whatever happened to be lying around the workshop. The less these disparate parts have to do with motorcycling, the better. If an old baked bean tin will serve in place of dealer supplied, factory-approved spare part, so much the better.

ABOVE **Indian custom bobber.** Bobbed, chopped, open-piped and with modern tyres – this old Indian side-valve has been through quite a few transformations over the years

LEFT **Billet handlebar grips** (just visible) are typical '90s extras on this typical '90s bike. Flat bars are a change from standard too

OVERLEAF **Ronald Torbich's Springer Softail** was two years in the making, and the changes are mostly subtle. The bike was Harley's most obvious attempt to cash in on the nostalgia boom

OPPOSITE Interesting tank mural on Mike Harding's Heritage – the four cylinders (two each side) show Knucklehead, Pan, Shovel and Evolution. Nice idea

OVERLEAF Harley's Heritage Softail apes the old Dresser look, and this one has many of the usual add-ons. Aftermarket air cleaner box, hub cover and sissy bar pad

CLASSICS – A result of the nostalgia boom (though have we ever lived in an age without nostalgia?), these take two forms, both based on a simple premise – how would bikers of forty or fifty years ago have customized their machines, given modern materials and know-how? There are those who try to make new bikes look old, usually Harleys, simply because the Milwaukee machines lend themselves to the treatment. Or it can be approached from the other direction, applying modern technology to bikes that really are old.

STREET – This can be the subtle end of customizing, with a superficially stock bike actually hiding quite extensive changes. More often though, it's a new paint job, with frame, forks and bodywork all much the same as when they left the factory.

TRIKES – Custom three-wheelers have become an integral part of the scene. At first sight, they seem to offer all the disadvantages of a car with none of the protection. But for customizers they offer a larger canvas, plus the opportunity to use much bigger engines – a V8 bike is unusable, but a V8 trike promises two-wheel performance for three or more people.

SCOOTERS – Not part of the American custom movement, but well established in Europe, especially the UK. Scooters seemed to fade from the scene in the early 1970s, but the Mod revival a few years later brought them back. (Harley-Davidson actually took a bath with their "Topper" scooter as early as 1960 – it's just not US style.) But in Europe, there is some serious customizing, with a lot of engraving and radical frame modifications on some bikes.

In other words, there's a lot more to custom bikes than something out of the movie *Easy Rider*. This blossoming of styles over the last decade or so has happened for one simple reason – interest in the custom movement has blossomed as well. You might think the mood of the 1990s, with its environmental concerns, and the threat of restrictive legislation, would discourage customizing. In fact, it seems to have done the opposite – in an increasingly secular, individualistic society, everyone seems to be searching for some other means of self-expression than what they do during office hours. Look at the burgeoning interest in the New Age and alternative religions, in 'adventure' holidays and specialist hobbies. The custom movement is just another manifestation of that – because each bike is its owner's personal creation. Even if it's only the addition of a few bolt-on accessories, it's all down to his or her choice, a reflection of individual tastes and needs.

And yet you rarely find this urge to customize anywhere else – there's still a custom car movement (but it isn't as thriving as the bikes are). There have been customized, low riding pedal cycles too. Originating from the Californian Chicano community, these have inspired some factory-built low riders, but have really never caught on beyond their Californian roots.

But otherwise, no other machine is personalised to the same extent. There are plenty of similar pastimes to motorcycling, like hang gliding and mountain biking, where the machine is an integral part of the activity. And as in motorcycling, the user's life depends on it. But these are seen more as tools, the means to an end. When not in use, the hang glider is folded up and forgotten. Every hang glider pilot

wants the best he or she can afford, but you won't see any with custom paintwork. It's not quite the same with mountain bikers – there is an accessories industry which will sell you flash-looking parts in purple anodised finish. But the real reason for buying these bits is that they are lighter or stronger than the standard version – the purple is nice, but it's not the raison d'être.

Motorbikes on the other hand, have instant visual appeal. Some say this is down to distant folk-memories of horse flesh, or perhaps because you can actually see the mechanical components. Unlike any other piece of machinery, where all the working parts are hidden away, on a motorcycle we can relate to the engine that powers it, the chain that takes power to the wheel, the suspension units that keep it off the ground. It's significant that even on the all-enveloping bodywork custom bikes, the engine is rarely covered up, it's the heart of the machine, a vital part of the whole display. And the recent trend towards covering up engines among the latest superbikes has come up against some market resistance. When Triumph bikes were relaunched in 1991, the 'naked' unfaired Trident was part of the range, and even the touring Trophy had a peephole in the fairing to give a glimpse of the engine and the promise of hidden power. Anyway, what comes out of all this speculation is one thing – people, not just bikers, love to stand and look at bikes. Customizing is an acceptance of that fact, and a celebration.

CHAPTER TWO

BOBBER TO CHOPPER

If you believe the history books, customizing was born as a result of a hyped-up 'riot' in Hollister, California, 1947. After Hollister, so the story goes, outlaw bikers coalesced into an alternative biking movement, of which customizing was an integral part. This version of events is true, but it's not the whole story – riders have been changing, or customizing, their bikes ever since motorcycles first turned a

RIGHT **Nice array of colours, kerbside at Sturgis, but a classic bobber on the left contrasts with heavy mudguarded compatriots. The bobbed rear 'guard, bare front wheel and drum brakes make it a real period piece**

wheel. What late forties California did see was the first signs of a conscious style – and as time went on, the style was pursued for its own sake, more so than for any practical advantages.

But even before the war, motorcyclists, in that endless quest for speed, were just as keen to swap bits around, modify some and ditch others altogether. These didn't always have a happy conclusion – one nameless rider in inter-war England shoe-horned a massive single (with equally massive external flywheel) into an empty

frame. All went well until he leaned over on the first corner – the impressive fly-wheel dug into the road and spat him off!

In the US, where horizons are further away, the 1920s saw the beginnings of the dresser style. To suit the long distances, screens, saddlebags and spotlights became de rigueur. The bikes (invariably Harley-Davidsons or Indians) were not modified at all, but there were approved accessories which added up to an overall look. Clubs grew up to cater for the tourists. They seem laughable now – if the pictures are any guide. Club members dressed up in smart, identical, military-style uniforms, and would ride two abreast in perfect forma-tion. Harley-Davidson loved the image they presented – in its ads, the square-jawed and very clean-cut riders partook in a whole-some, healthy, "outdoor pursuit". Clubmen and women were neat, clean and presentable. They wore ties and pleasant smiles. They did good works. And they were about to get a nasty shock.

This was where Hollister came in. There was another breed of biker, very different to the uniformed Mouseketeers. Many of them were ex-GIs, fresh back from the har-rowing experience of war in Europe. Some had ridden bikes in the army, which used Harleys throughout the war as couriers, or on reconaissance. They came home in 1945 to find America had moved on - those who stayed behind had moved on too, into the best jobs. And although American industry had done well out of the war, that didn't mean prosperity for all. The gap between rich and poor was as big as ever. Even if they did find work, for some ex-ser-vicemen, civilian life was simply too boring. So they got on their Harleys and went on the road.

RIGHT **It may look like a repainted XLCR, but Donnie Smith's Sportster was actually an XLCH which he took three months to street racerize. The engine has been opened up to 84ci**

But life with the respectable clubs would have been too regimented – too much like the army. Instead, they formed gangs with names like Satan's Sinners. Tieless and scruffy, they would roar out into the countryside, doing their best to offend middle America. More to the point from our point of view, they all liked to modify their bikes in the same way. These boys were less concerned with a neat image than with speed and power, and there they had a problem. Harleys of the time were outdated and slow, especially compared with the increasing numbers of British bikes which were now reaching the US market – 15,000 were sold in 1947, three-quarters of H-D's entire production that year. The Triumphs, Nortons and BSAs didn't have long distance stamina, but compared to a lumbering V-twin they were quick, neat

back was chopped or 'bobbed' to a much shorter length – the California Bobber was born. None of this made the V-twins as nimble as a Norton, but it did make them a little faster in a straight line. Just as important, the California Bobber look was stripped down, lean and mean, worlds away from the dressers. It also became associated with a certain sort of biker.

About 500 of these unshaven types turned up at Hollister for an AMA race meeting, along with over 3,000 cleaner cut bikers who, according to the AMA "parked their equipment and registered at local hotels for a good night's sleep". Apparently the trouble started when local residents poured something unspeakable out of a first floor window, onto the heads of those bikers who didn't want a good night's sleep. Trouble ensued, though it was far from the reign of terror which subsequent press reports detailed.

In fact, by noon the following day just 29 cops had restored order. What arrests there were, were for drunkeness, indecent exposure and traffic fines. No evidence of devil worship or chickens having their heads bitten off. But the nation's reporters were in no mood to let the facts spoil a good story – as far as they were concerned, 4,000 bikers had taken over the town amid anarchic scenes of wild excess. In those McCarthyite days, it was another threat to the American Way of Life, truly the enemy within. The AMA rallied round, closed ranks and generally made it clear that the 'one percenter' troublemakers had nothing to do with law-abiding motorcyclists.

Anyway, the importance of Hollister was not what really happened there, but the after effect, the coverage it gave to the gangs, their bikes and way of life. When the

and incredibly nimble. How could the Harleys keep up?

Tuning was expensive and largely confined to the race track, so Harley riders did the next best thing, and started to trim weight off their bikes. Screens were junked, as were footboards and sometimes the front brake as well. The front mudguard went (in sunny California they could afford to do without it) and that on the

RIGHT **Six years after Hollister** *The Wild One* **hit screens as a thinly veiled (and of course totally inaccurate) re-enactment. "What are you rebelling against Johnny?" "What have you got?"**

Establishment AMA entreated kids not to do this at home, naturally it had the opposite effect. Suddenly, bike gangs and the California Bobber look were spreading right across the US, far from their West Coast origins. The custom movement was born.

CHOP EVOLUTION

If Hollister was the birth of this alternative biking scene (to which customizing was inextricably linked) then Stanley Kramer's *The Wild One* was the first milestone. His 1953 film was thought so shocking and rabble rousing that many authorities banned it outright – it was twenty years before the UK censors thought they could trust the British public to watch it! It was basically a very loose dramatisation of what happened at Hollister – bikes rode into bars and their riders caused havoc. The action centred around the rivalry between two bike gangs led respectively by Lee Marvin (chopped Harley) and Marlon Brando (stock Triumph).

For the first time on celluloid, all the bad guys rode bikes; that was part of what defined them. The motorcycle had been used sporadically on film before, representing danger, death and the modern world, but not as so obvious a harbinger of subversion. Compare the Brando movie to the English George Formby's *No Limit*, made in 1935 – there were some dastardedly villains on bikes, but so was our George, the perennial cheeky chappy. Whatever Kramer's motives, *The Wild One* had the effect of spreading the news of bad boy biker gangs and their stripped down bikes still further, and of popularising them. Motorcycles were no longer just working-class transport, they were a symbol

LEFT Harley's side-valve 45 engine powered thousands of Servicars and WLA army bikes, but was never very fast. Turbocharging is one (extreme) solution

of rebellion. As the 1950s progressed, and car ownership became a viable option for many more people, the motorcycle's role as cheap, simple transport mutated into this very different image.

By the time people were queuing up to watch *The Wild One*, the Bobber look was well established. It had ended up as a replica of racing bikes such as the Harley WR – no front mudguard and chopped down rear, open pipes and no front brake. WRs were the standard hillclimb competitor; long, steep hillclimbs, in which very few riders actually reached the top, had replaced the board tracks, whose splinter injuries made the high speeds doubly dangerous.

In fact, competition was to give the spur for the next change in the look of the early custom. In 1952, Harley finally replaced its hopelessly outclassed WR racer with the partially up-to-date KR. The well known rider Billy Kuber took the unusual step of replacing his new KR's 4-gallon fuel tank with the tiny 2-gallon one from the 125cc Harley Hummer.

The Hummer incidentally, was one of H-D's numerous attempts to break into the market for little bikes. Based, like BSA's Bantam, on a pre-war two-stroke DKW, it was not a huge success, but its fuel tank was to live on. Billy Kuber presumably fitted the Hummer tank to save weight, but it also completely changed the look of any bike. Its small size made the engine look bigger (a good thing) and exposed more frame to accentuate the stripped down look (another good thing). Customizers loved the effect it gave, and soon small tanks became part of the accepted look. Those big fat gas tanks smacked too much of the comfortable tourist. Even Harley-Davidson Motor Co took note, and when the new Sportster was launched in 1957, the high compression, light weight XLCH used one of the tiny tanks to good effect.

As the fifties progressed, the chop look kept on evolving; though it was now drag racing which took a hand. There had always been drag racing, often of the unofficial after-midnight sort on public roads.

RIGHT The V-twin is an 80ci version with Dell 'Orto twin choke carburettor. Carburettor changes are often among the first steps in upgrading a standard Harley

RIGHT This Sportster was originally built by Mark Shadley. Mike Estabrooks finished it to come second at the '83 Rat's Hole Show

LEFT Another low riding
Sportster, this time based
on a 1962 bike which was
customized in '83. Spare,
open style echoes the
earliest bobbers

But now it was being organized. And the more competitive it got, the more specialised the bikes had to be to achieve a good time on the standing quarter. Rigid rear ends, a lowered frame and raked out front forks all helped keep the front end on the tarmac and the bike more stable. Gradually, the drag strip look began to creep into customizing, and a new look began to develop. The lower, hardtail rear end, with fat rear tyre, plus a skinny tyre at the front, were all straight from drag racing. Customizers were helped by the many suppliers in California who had grown up to sell to racers, but now found themselves selling frames, tanks and tuning parts for road bikes as well.

What the customizers *weren't* trying to do was simply copy the drag racers – they just took the bits they wanted, and as a new decade dawned, were adding ideas of their

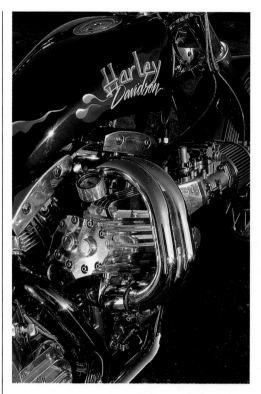

own. The most obvious were the lengthened girder forks – Harley's own telescopic forks, which had been around since the late 1940s, just made the whole bike look squat and dumpy, which didn't fit in with the rangy skeleton that most customizers wanted - customizing was still close to its roots of stripping down to shed weight, and longer forks looked the part.

At first, the extensions were home made, but soon any number of firms were offering ready-made extended forks, from three inches longer than stock to sixteen, eighteen or more. The old girder forks weren't as comfortable as hydraulics, but they were a lot easier to cut in half and extend. Anyway, those gaunt tubes sticking out in front of the bike looked just right. Often there was no attempt to rake the forks out, so the longer ones made the whole bike point skywards. There were old V-twin wives' tales that this would starve the front (higher) cylinder of oil, but Harley owners

needn't have worried, as the dry sump system kept pumping lube round regardless of the angle.

Still, there was an answer, which soon became an integral part of the look. The frame was raked, to put the forks out at a greater angle and keep everything on a more even keel – serious frame modifications had arrived. The principle behind it was simple. Just cut an inch or two out of the top frame tube, heat up the down tube and bend it back until the top tube closed together again for rewelding. If that wasn't enough, you could have the whole frame stretched, which again emphasised the stretched out, skeletal outline of the classic chopper. And just as for any other serious

LEFT Dragster for the road. Looks are part and parcel of serious drag bikes, and this one is no exception – the big twin choke carburettor is shown off to good effect

BELOW, LEFT Arvid Albanese's drag bike was built for fast quarter mile times, but it sill uses paintwork to suggest speed and movement

OPPOSITE **Before paint became important, custom bikes were measured by the height of the handlebars, or so it seems now, looking back**

RIGHT **Hardtail rear ends can have an unfortunate effect on the rider!**

BELOW, RIGHT **Classic 1970s chop with radical riding position and raked frame. Now that Springer front forks are the favourite for raking, those thickset telescopics look a bit awkward**

engineering change, to be safe, it had to be done properly. Maybe it was some of the home-made backyard specials that got custom bikes a bad name, but it also created an opportunity for professional customizers to set up. Soon, there were shops all over the US that would do anything to your bike - hardtail it, rake the forks, supply chopped mudguards or Hummer tanks.

The handlebars evolved to suit the new scrawny shape - you could buy risers to raise the standard bars, or better still some more radical high-rise bars, which eventually became ultra-high ape-hangers. At the other end of the bike, simple handholds grew skywards to complement them. The long, tall sissy bar had arrived. Anyway, this tail-down, hands in the air look marked the arrival of the classic chopper. Ed Roth went on nationwide TV to explain, "Chopping is the latest addition to folk art – the creative espression of a motorcycle-borne generation."

And it was definitely an *American* folk-art. In the UK and Europe, riders were customizing their bikes in completely different ways. During the 1950s and '60s, just as the chopper was becoming the American custom bike, so the café racer

OVERLEAF **Rat's Hole Show competitor in 1978. Lots of bodywork changes to this bike, which was actually built a few years earlier**

OPPOSITE **Brian Bussaglia's FLH looks about to be engulfed by the sea as the tide comes in at Daytona. Ape hangers live!**

was doing the same in Britain. It was really down to racing – in Britain, circuit racing was the thing, whether on the legendary Isle of Man course or short circuits like Thruxton and Goodwood. So the natural thing was to make your bike look like it had just come back from a record lap. The emphasis was on speed and handling, just the thing for Britain's narrow twisting 'A' and 'B' roads. But in the States, where drag

ABOVE, RIGHT **Shovel-headed Harley choppers, waiting at the lights in Daytona. SU carburettor is often chosen for its looks, though it's good for fuel economy as well**

RIGHT **Two V-twins, one customized, at the V-Twin Rally in Shaftesbury, England. Parading through the hill-top town is a favourite pastime**

RIGHT It was once a police bike (1979), now transformed by the flames, bars and Ness accessories

BELOW An awful lot of people who have never ridden so much as a Honda step-thru would take a guess that this is Peter Fonda's Panhead chop from *Easy Rider*. They would be wrong. It is in fact an incredible 1990s replica built by Jim Leonard in Valencia Ca. using a 1954 1200 cc engine and 1962 bottom end. It's kind of a fake of a fake! Don't think about it too hard, you'll go dizzy

racing and hill climbs were bigger influences, and roads were straight and long, the chopper was the result.

In 1969 came 'official' confirmation of the chopper's existence. *Easy Rider*, in which Peter Fonda and Dennis Hopper cruised across the States along endless empty blacktops, did the same job for chops as *The Wild One* had for Bobbers just sixteen years before. Like the Brando bandwagon, it drew on a customizing style which had been around for a while, but popularised it, bringing it to the attention of a far wider audience outside the bike fraternity. Indeed, that one film is often cited

as the main reason for Britain's catching on to the chopper look (or 'craze' as it was called at the time) in 1969-70. But there were also important differences between the two films. In *The Wild One*, bikers were black-hats, pure and simple (with the exception of Brando's 'heart of gold' character), but Hopper and Fonda were free-wheeling heroes, facing a redneck world of prejudice and hatred.

This was all very well. The trouble was, by the time *Easy Rider* was released, the chops it portrayed had hardly changed in almost a decade. The custom bike seemed to have reached its definitive form – most customizers seemed to agree that chops looked good, but that was it. Where to go from here? Well, if long forks looked good, then longer ones must look even better. So, year on year, forks, bars and rake grew longer, taller and more extreme. It was really a substitute for progress, just more of the same.

SHOW TIME

The bikes were certainly an eyeful; the trouble was, they weren't very nice to ride. Peter Fonda was later to admit that, though the chop he rode in *Easy Rider* looked terrific, it was anything but an easy-riding bike, especially when Jack Nicholson was on pillion.

Dennis Hopper's bike on the other hand, was more restrained. With standard rake forks and flat bars on risers, it was closer to the old Bobber look, and probably easier to ride as a result. Maybe it wasn't just coincidence that only Hopper performed in-saddle antics on-screen, while Captain America seemed reluctant to rise out of his seat.

Of course, this didn't matter if the chop had been built purely to compete in custom shows. The pure show bike had arrived, and as the 1960s ended, some began to question what all this had to do with motorcycling. John Reed (better known as Uncle Bunt) the English builder of customs, later recalled an incident in the States. One of his bikes had just won a show, but a cynical bystander challenged him to actually ride it. Reed hopped on and roared off, point proven, only to find the brakes didn't work – he had filled the hydraulics with vegetable oil, proper brake fluid might have damaged the paintwork!

Uncle Bunt was one of the high profile customizers, but for most riders, customizing was a lot less ambitious. And as the decade turned, there were an awful lot of them around. The first custom bike magazine (*Super Cycle*) hit US shelves in 1968; soon there were others, and every one was stuffed with adverts from the custom industry. And it had become an industry. Quite apart from the existing purveyors of frames and tanks, a new breed of bolt-on merchant was springing up. Not everyone had the money, inclination or ability to make their bike a radical custom. More to the point, they had to ride the bike to work on Monday, so it couldn't be taken off the road for months of transformation work.

The answer was bolt-on parts. Tail lights in the shape of Maltese crosses or swastikas (the same went for mirrors). If the peanut tank was a little common these days, you could buy one in the shape of a coffin. Oil tanks were easy to swap too – these also came in coffin shapes, as well as hexagons, and countless other variations. Bolting on 'custom' parts was quick, cheap and satisfying (for the owner, at the very least). Well,

not always quick – some of these parts were sold mail order, sight unseen, and weren't as bolt-on as the ads suggested: "Designed to bolt right on, AND THEY FIT!!" There was a new craze for chroming as well, another quick transformation job.

But even if your coffin tank and Maltese mirror did fit, they didn't make your bike a custom, because thousands of other riders had bought exactly the same parts. Customizing was almost becoming too easy, and custom bikes seemed to be running towards a dead end.

Even the more radical bikes, the real customs which had been rebuilt from scratch, looked little different to what was doing the rounds last year. Someone had to come up with something new.

CHAPTER THREE
BORN AGAIN CUSTOMS

In 1970, the average custom bike seemed stuck in a time warp. If customizing was going to survive, it had to develop. Like any art form, the energy came from new ideas. Fortunately, that was what it got. There was a new emphasis on paintwork and engraving (at first just as a means of tarting up the old chop), and complete new styles of bike did emerge. Custom builders became more concerned about rideability (though the pure show bike continued to flourish). Clever detailing is now often as important as the overall look. Quality and workmanship is admired. Perhaps most important of all, there are no rules about how a custom bike should look. The only limit is the owner/builder's own imagination.

This has brought tremendous health, vitality and variety to the custom movement. So much so that in 1994 something called 'BikeArt' was held in Birmigham, England. It was an exhibition of some of the best (and one of the worst) examples of customizing, from chops and café racers to futuristic bikes a long way from the traditional custom. The point was not just the variety of bikes on show, nor just that the public was invited in to have a good look. It was an acceptance by part of the mainstream art

OPPOSITE 'Deanager' won Best Paint & Chrome (Dresser) at the Rat's Hole Show in Daytona recently. You can see why

RIGHT The secret of any ultimate custom is stunning looks as well as technical specifications – note the close fitting bodywork and twin six-pot brake callipers at the rear of this bike

RIGHT "I wouldn't have built the bike just for show, so everything had to work, and work well" – Richard Taylor

world that custom bikes were in themselves an art form, and a vibrant, thriving one.

Michael Diamond, Director of the gallery where BikeArt was held: "There is a marvellous openness about the aesthetics of custom biking; an openness to stimulation from a wide range of visual sources; an openness to the idea that anything can be used in any way you like (and you are the only judge that matters); an openness to the idea that good work is not restricted to those with formal qualifications or other symbols of status. There is passion too; passion in the love of certain kinds of imagery; passion in the commitment to master craft skills without formal training; passion in the belief in the need to express your own

values in a world of bland conformity." Phew, a lot of words about a touch of candy paint, but he's right.

LOWRIDER

This was all very different to the days when there was just one type of custom bike, so how did it happen? The lowrider had a lot to do with it, inspiring builders to widen their horizons. Just as the first chops had come out of Calfornia, so did this. Arlen Ness (if Ed Roth was the Grandaddy of US customizing, then Ness was and is a favourite uncle) is usually credited with having kicked things off with his Bay Area Lowriders of the early 1970s.

The inspiration came from drag racing, where in the never-ending race to lop another hundredth off the standing quarter, bikes were geting lower and longer. While chops became ever more laid-back, the drag bikes that helped to inspire them had gone the other way.

So lowriders for the street still had stretched frames and raked forks, but the forks were often standard length, and the bars, rather than pointing towards the sky,

BELOW **A contrast –** spindly Springer contrasts in every way imaginable against a bodywork bike. The latter's clean, simple paint job, and solid wheels, are typical

BOTTOM **This Springer** could have been named The Zebra, but wasn't. Twin level pipes accentuate the spindly look, and there are too many add-ons to list

swept back horizontally towards the rider, tiller fashion. Or else they were simple flat bars that had the rider stretched out over the tank, mimicking the drag rider's stance. Bikes like this were lower and more stable than the average chop, so they could handle more power. That in turn allowed tuning, with speed as the object, to creep back into customizing.

It soon became clear that lowriders weren't going to stagnate – there are now several variations on the theme, all of which are still appearing as new bikes. The long, low minimalist lowrider was really the original, an example being Uncle Bunt's Roadrunner of 1977. It happened when tyre makers Avon asked him to build something to show off its latest rubber. And Bunt (who has done more than any other English customizer to translate American styles across the Atlantic) obliged. He used a Triumph twin engine, which naturally lent itself to the bike's lean, narrow look. Now of course, lowriders are powered by just about any type of engine you care to name, but a vertical twin or a V is the classic thing to use. More recently, we've seen the stubbier, fatter form of lowrider. Less

radical than the long and rangey style, these sit you just as low, but with a standard tank, no fork rake and flat bars. The idea is to get away from the skeletal outline of the classic dragster inspired bike to something more solid-looking.

In the early eighties came a third variation, the street racer. It was really lowrider meets café racer, with tuning, headlamp fairing and the emphasis on performance. It was a blending of styles which showed up something new in the custom movement – a willingness to borrow ideas from wherever they happened to be.

THE FACTORY ANGLE

Of course, the lowrider's ultimate acceptance came when Harley-Davidson named one of its production bikes after the style. Which brings us to factory customs. Just like the original lowrider and its offshoots, the factory custom has done much to reinvigorate the whole custom movement, bringing in riders who otherwise wouldn't have dreamed of owning anythng but a very conventional bike. Still, it sounds like

LEFT Tommy Jansson built this lowrider himself over five months. Bob Gorske of Roade Studio did the paint (red with yellow candy shadows) and the high compression engine features Andrews cams

RIGHT Understated red and silver on black complements the engraving by the prolific Dave Perewitz

BELOW, RIGHT Classic low rider, by Mark Shadley, though by the time this one was third at the 1983 Rat's Hole, the style was well established

LEFT This bike started out
as a 1970 Sportster, but
twelve years later was
transformed by Cycle Fab

OPPOSITE **Typicial 1970s chop from Cycle Fab shows the classic tiny tank with abundant painting, plating and engraving: excessive decoration of the functional object, or art? "The function of art is to break the monopoly upon that which is real." (Anton Ehrenzweig). "Yeah, whatever." (Dave Perewitz)**

TOP, LEFT **Brakes and forks come from a Honda, but Dave Perewitz's engraving does much to disguise the fact, as do the gold plated rims**

TOP, RIGHT **As usual, Dave Perewitz did the paint on Cycle Fab's behalf, with a design which extends the swirly engraved theme**

LEFT **Every conceivable part has been engraved or enhanced in some way, with the possible exception of the chain**

HARLEY-DAVIDSON FXRS

Builder	Battistinis
Owner	Nick Holmes
Engine	Air-cooled V-twin (1991 Harley Evo)
Barrels	H-D
Capacity	1490cc (89ci)
Cylinder heads	Modified H-D
Pistons	S&S
Camshaft	Crane 286
Crankshaft	S&S
Carburettor	S&S Super E
Air cleaner	Ness Billet Air Scoop
Ignition	MC Power Arc Single Fire
Exhaust system Pipes Silencers	Thunder Header Rich
Primary drive	Chain/M6 tensioner
Clutch	H-D
Gearbox	5-speed H-D
Brakes Front Rear	Twin 4-pot Billet calipers Single 4-pot Billet caliper
Suspension Front Rear	H-D forks, Ness Wide Glide yokes, detailing kit, progressive springs Fournales shocks, Ness twin rail swinging arm
Frame	H-D FXRS, standard rake

Japanese factory custom of about fifteen years ago – slightly higher bars, a stepped seat and a splash of extra chrome were considered enough to make anything 'customized'.

Things are different now. There's enough demand for the Japanese factories to produce custom-specific frames and engines – thumping 650cc singles, even massive V-twins to out-Harley Harley. Not that factory customs are new. Back in 1970, Triumph commissioned Craig Vetter to do a thorough restyling job on its Trident, transforming the square-rigged triple into a lovely three-piped swoop of a machine. At about the same time there was the Harley

a real contradiction in terms, as surely nothing to emerge off a production line can be 'custom' in any sense of the word. That was certainly true of the typical

LEFT **Plain black is still favoured by some, though in the case of Nick Holmes' Battistini-built FXR, it could be to emphasize the engine. That's been enlarged to 1,490cc, thanks to S&S crank, con-rods and pistons**

SuperGlide, H-D's final recognition of what people had been doing to its bikes for years. And it's Harley which has made a real success of factory customs, in two ways.

First, it has consciously designed certain bikes to echo certain custom looks. The Low Rider we've already mentioned, but there's also the Softail, which gives a hardtail look but with full rear suspension. Springer forks are technically outmoded, but they've long been a favourite with customizers, so Harley brought out a modern lookalike version.

This of course is only part of the story. For most riders, it still isn't enough to buy a ready-made custom, there has to be something about it you've done yourself, something which marks it out as your bike. As Richard La Plante wrote in his book *Hog Fever*, "Anyone riding a stock Harley 'doesn't know'. Doesn't know that the whole idea of buying a Harley is to take it apart and change things. To personalise it, give it some identity, make it unique. Stock bikes are boring."

That's why H-D now sells a vast range of customizing parts, from 'Live to Ride' points covers to serious engine tuning under the Screamin' Eagle trade name. Parts manufacturers like Custom Chrome and Drag Specialities, long in the business of custom add-ons for Harleys, have also

OPPOSITE **Somewhere underneath all that is a V-twin, but it's long since lost the battle for attention with the outrageous carb stacks and supercharger**

TOP, RIGHT **Not quite as outrageous, but painting the carburettor body to match the bike makes a certain statement as well**

BOTTOM, RIGHT **In customizing terms, superchargers have two jobs to do: one is to boost performance, the other is the far more important task, to many, of looking good**

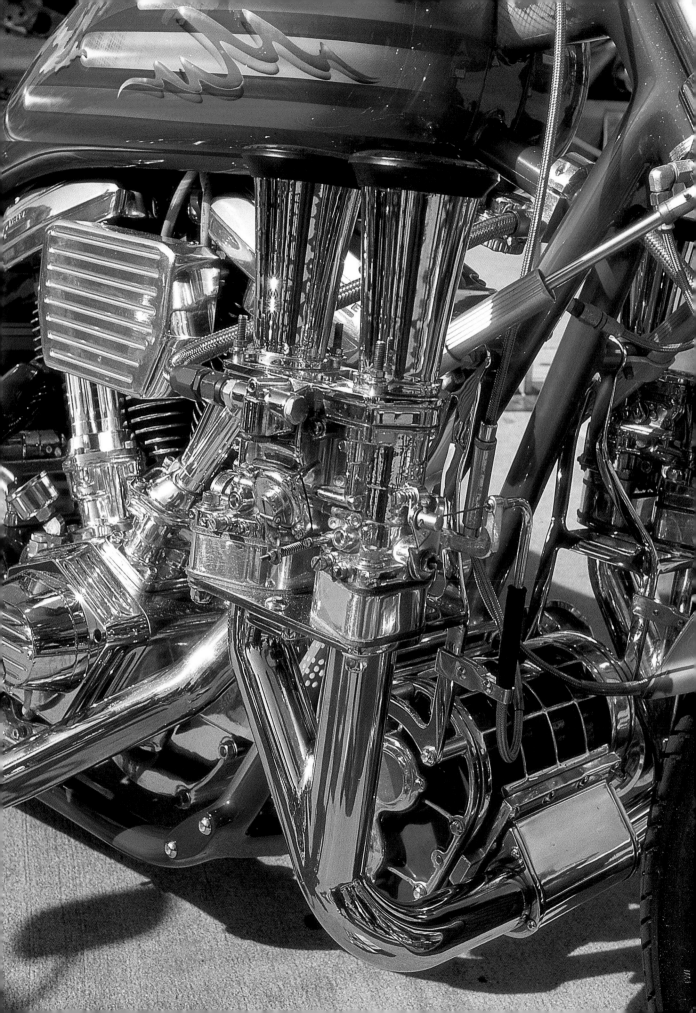

RIGHT **Nineties style custom Harley on Main Street, Sturgis, with typical high-price add-ons**

BELOW, LEFT **Nice paint on display outside the Boot Hill Saloon in Daytona – and not a Japanese bike in sight**

BELOW, RIGHT **More tassles in the dresser tradition – with chrome studs, pillion pad and fishtail silencers on this example too**

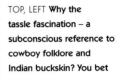

TOP, LEFT **Why the tassle fascination – a subconscious reference to cowboy folklore and Indian buckskin? You bet**

LEFT **If you were in any doubt … Harley-Davidsons are American motorcycles. The paint here is by John McCarthy, and the bike is owned by Bernie Tatro**

BELOW, LEFT **Traditional treatment for this Shovelhead – duotone colour scheme, eagle's wing and handlebar tassles. 'Live to Ride' air cleaner box isn't particularly radical either**

RIGHT Jim Randolph's '93 FXR Superglide shows a variety of custom skills and parts. St Paul H-D built the engine, and it's a standard 80ci with HeadQuarters cam, ported heads with oversize valves, and Screamin' Eagle ignition

benefitted. Many people want to customize their bikes, but are happy with no more than a different air cleaner cover and new set of pipes – it's really the old bolt-on business again. As Harleys have become fashionable, so has the business of step-by-step customizing.

NOSTALGIA & THE LINERS

Harleys being the beasts they are, much of this customizing has to do with making the bike look older than it really is. This is really a whole new custom style, another way in which the whole process has found new life. The Springer front forks are straight out of the twenties, while the Heritage Softail opts for an early fifties Hydraglide look. And it's not just Harley doing it. The reborn Triumph, with a name at least as old as H-D's has just launched the Thunderbird, basically its standard frame and three cylinder engine topped by 1950s bodywork.

But away from the factories, there are plenty of other customs which look to the past for inspiration. Take Dan Wilson's Classified Motorcycle Co, which converted H-D Sportsters into Vincent Rapides. All it took was a new seat, tank, bars and mudguards, plus the right detailing. So close was it to the original (even the tank badge was modelled on the famous Vincent one) that you'd have to get pretty close to tell them apart. Still, it's unlikely that Dan ever ventured into a HOG meeting on the bike, let alone a gathering of Vincents … The Goodman HDS was a more modern version of the same thing - the Goodman brothers in England built replicas of the legendary Norton Featherbed frame, and

OVERELEAF A slightly older Harley this one, a 1979 FLH of the pre-Evo era. As a custom though, it's right up to date

OVERELEAF, INSET Tom Fedorowski of White Bear Lake, Minnesota, is the bike's builder as well as the owner

old. Paul Brierly's BSA A10 (which was displayed at BikeArt) was updated with monoshock rear suspension, plus lots of stainless steel and polished alloy. It's an interesting idea. How would bikers of forty or fifty years ago have customized their bikes, given modern paint, materials and know-how?

There's one other aspect to the backwards-looking custom. Customizing has been going for so long now, that it's begun to develop its very own nostalgia. The old styles are coming back. Danny Franssen's Bobber echoes the very early Californian customs, with its Springer forks and bobbed rear mudguard. The frame is an authentic Hydraglide rigid item, and the tank's a period piece too, but a new Evo V-twin and classy modern (black and blue) paintwork mark this out as a nineties bike. Apehangers, inevitably, have come back

OPPOSITE **Aeroquip** hoses have long been a custom builder's favourite, and blend in well with the 'engineering' milled-from-solid look favoured by many

LEFT **Nice** chrome edging to finish off this rear end, which is lowered by three inches. The frame is also raked by ten degrees, but engine is mostly standard

BELOW, LEFT **Standard** fatbob tank, but finished in Candy Purple with Pearl White and Candy Blue graphics of the Kerpow! variety. Dash is a Custom Chrome one

shoehorned the Sportster V-twin into some of them. With up-to-date cycle parts, it made a truly modern café racer, though it looked older.

Individual builders too, have gone for the nostalgia look. It might be just a duo-tone paint job to make a Heritage Softail look like something out of the fifties. But you can go a lot further. One Sportster owner transformed his bike with big, wide mudguards, shortened rear shocks, single seat and dash-mounted Hydraglide speedometer. And of course, the specialists are quite happy to supply all the right bits - Lawayne Matthies (Xzotic Cycle Products) has specialised in ribbed generator covers, headlamp nacelles and kits to make an Evo engine look like a Panhead.

An alternative to making a new bike look old is to approach things from the other direction – modernise a bike that really is

ABOVE **Bodywork bikes don't always work, especially when the engine is covered up. It seems to defeat the whole object of having a motorcycle in the first place – slab-sided panels don't help either**

RIGHT **One has to ask why bother, though somebody somewhere spent a long time building this bike. But what right have we to carp? That's part of the joy of customizing. As Donald Trump (probably) said, "Beauty is in the eye of the freeholder."**

contemporary any more. But if anyone can influence a new interest in certain chopper styling cues, it's high profile figures like Arlen Ness. Ness built two bikes to publicise his new Taildragger mudguards. They were low-slung, ground-hugging machines which emphasised the taildragging look. But up front a set of apehangers pointed towards the sky, making a real hybrid of two styles.

Bodywork bikes, or luxury liners as they're sometimes called, are more of a 1990s thing, but here too there are nods to the past. The idea is to produce an elegant, opulent cruiser, the complete opposite of the lean and hungry custom which was the rule for so long. Huge valanced mudguards are obligatory, to the extent that the rear wheel is almost totally enclosed. These swooping 'guards are there to emphasis the bike's length and movement, and they are inspired by none other than the Indian Chief - the custom movement is not governed by the past, but the past

too. Brian Bussaglia fitted them to his ex-police FLH, but with standard frame and forks. Choppers, it seems, are not making a comeback, simply because they never went away – like traditional jazz, they've always been with us, even if they aren't actually

often provides its inspiration. The forks are sometimes raked (though they are seldom much longer than standard) and the frame may be stretched, again to emphasise length. Wheels are often solid rather than spoked, and there's usually a nacelle fairing as well. A few builders have even taken bodywork to its logical conclusion and enclosed the engine as well. Fortunately, this hasn't caught on. I say fortunately because to hide away the engine seems to take away the chief reason for customizing a bike in the first place. Liner paintwork is usually understated and dark, but very glossy, with chrome highlights. So far, the liner look has been mainly favoured by American and French builders, and there's no doubt it's here to stay.

There's one aspect to these modern bikes that comes up again and again: billet parts. Carved from solid chunks of alloy, these have been made possible by relatively affordable computer controlled CNC lathes. These let the operator produce

ABOVE Fat Slug is a French custom, and perhaps a better interpretation of bodywork than the previous attempt. It was built by Odessey Kolours for Freeway magazine, and features a Cyberdyne digital speedomete

LEFT Few engine mods (apart from cosmetic ones) and despite its radical appearance, Fat Slug (which appeared at the '94 Rat's Hole) used several off-the-shelf parts – mudguards, lights, bars and grips were all from Arlen Ness

one-off parts or batches with terrific accuracy, and they can be any shape or size you want. In other words, perfect for the world of customizing. A solid wheel? No problem. Handlebar grips and footrests? A cinch. Perhaps the most common are

OPPOSITE Interesting tank design here, incorporating bright colours, traditional skulls and mechanical images

RIGHT The first thing most Harley owners change are the brakes, which haven't kept up with the rest of the bike – Billet or PM callipers are popular uprates

BELOW, This is an Evo V-twin, but the ribbed primary cover makes it look older

brake calipers, which actually have the trade name Billet - they're most common on expensive custom Harleys, whose factory brakes not only don't work too well, but look rather puny into the bargain. Billet parts have transformed customizing in recent years; not only do they gave great freedom to the builder who wants (and can afford) a one-off part that nobody else has, but the 'mass-produced' bits are high quality items, guaranteed to fit every time. It's a long way from the shoddy accessories of twenty years ago.

The downside is that none of this is cheap – large chunks of aluminium have never been bargain priced – but it really has transformed the top end of customizing. The big US custom houses now sell huge ranges of billet parts, and the whole thing has revitalised the bolt-on business as well as the money-no-object end of things. It's even contributed to a new look. Carved alloy looks so good on its own, that it is rarely painted. Even things like handlebar grips are being left with as burnished alloy. It's a sort of 'engineering' look, a sheen rather than shine. If you must have colour, then alloy can be anodised, which again gives a different look to traditional paint. But billet parts are just the latest new technique – the more traditional tools of customizing have been developing too.

HARLEY-DAVIDSON
FXRLC

Builder/Owner	Mallard Teal
Engine	Air cooled V-twin (1987 H-D Evo)
Capacity	1340cc
Cylinder barrels	H-D, 0.030" over size
Pistons	H-D, 10.5:1 cr
Cylinder heads	Rev Tech
Camshaft	Sifton
Carburettor	Mikuni
Ignition	Points
Exhaust system	Python II
Other engine modificatons	Nitrous oxide injection
Clutch	Barnet
Gearbox	Andrews
Brakes	
Front	GMA
Rear	GMA
Suspension	
Front	Stock H-D telescopic forks
Rear	Fournales air shock
Wheels	
Front	PM 21"
Rear	PM 18"
Frame	H-D, 5 degree rake, ½" stretch, fully moulded
Paint	
Colour	Red/Purple/Silver
Designer/Painter	Mallard Teal

Special thanks to Don & Lee Tima, Payne Ave Body Shop, Deborah Pearson

MINNESOTA
13-366 c
10,000 LAKES

CHAPTER FOUR
PAINT & METAL

Luxury liners, billet footrests, nostalgia and sophisticated engineering - it's all a far cry from the late '60s, when paint was the only way of making your chop look different to all the others. But despite everything else, paint is still central to any custom bike. Flames were always a popular theme, lifted from the world of hot rodding. The story goes that one car burst into flames when half way down the drag strip, thus providing the inspiration for thousands of car and bike painters ever since. It's the combination of a sense of movement and hint of danger that makes them still popular today. Now of course, the flames are stylised things, as often purple or green as the traditional orange-red. but though the techniques are more sophisticated, the idea hasn't changed.

In fact, paint itself has developed to allow ever more intricate designs. Two pack paints give a cleaner, brighter colour (simple solid colours are making a comeback now) and can be lacquered to give a deep quality finish. Metallics were the first innovation though, with their tiny flakes of aluminium to give some authentic flash. Just like the extreme chops, some people tended to use metalflake paint to excess – combining garish colours and acres of chrome to build a tinsel tree on wheels. No part of the bike was safe. Satin paint ('Sock 'Em with Satins!' suggested the subtly worded ads of the time) soon followed, though

it never had such a wide following. Now there is a bewildering range of paints on offer. Pearlescents give a fairly opaque, pearl-like finish; candies give tone to a background design; neon paint is great for day-glo colours. Other advances have made it easier for home customizers to achieve quite sophisticated effects. A good example is spray-on masking. You just spray the stuff on, like paint, and once dry, it leaves a thin rubbery film all over the painted surface. You then draw on the pattern you want, cut along the line with a modellers' knife and peel away the masking you don't need. Finally, spray over the top in whatever colour you fancy. Simple (in theory).

OPPOSITE **Some painters display great imagination and originality in creating new designs; others prefer a more traditional theme; originality is not in itself an automatically superior option. Why the mildly customized Springer Softail on its way past the camping ground in South Dakota en route to Daytona? Erm, some booksellers can get a little censorious**

ABOVE, RIGHT **The days of the big bad black bike may still be with us, but there are plenty of alternatives now, as shown by this pink-framed Evo with its air-brushed tank**

RIGHT **In the US, Harley-Davidson dominates the world of customizing; and despite Japanese factory customs and some marvellous machinery born out of other makes, so it does in the rest of the world**

Designs too, have come a long way since the flames, as well all that gothic imagery of ruined castles, monstrous fanged snakes and muscular naked women (of physically unfeasible proportions). Without getting too pretentious, the mock Gothic/Medieval imagery is surely something to do with knights on horseback associations, whether Lancelot or Mordred, firing up the V-twin in pursuit of some undefined American Holy Grail. Now, murals, graphics and patterns, even straight copies of Old Masters, have all been made possible by the airbrush. This is quite simply a smaller, finer version of the

standard spray gun, which allows a great delicacy in the work. It's become an art in itself, allowing the painter to build up layer upon layer to give an overall richness and depth which earlier bike artists could only dream of. Murals took advantage of this, to reach a peak in the late seventies/early eighties, when it seemed no custom was complete without its own example of tank art.

Things have moved on since then. Look at a modern gathering of custom bikes, and you'll see a good sprinkling of flames, bulging torsos and red-eyed vampires. But in keeping with the greater variety of bikes,

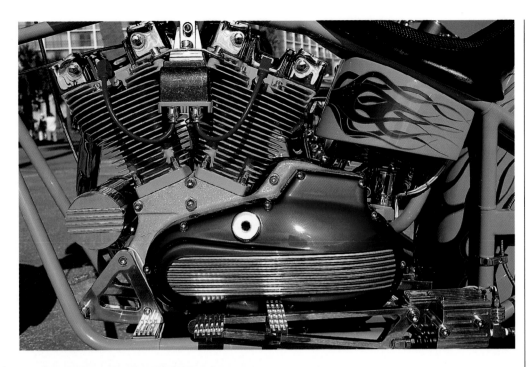

OPPOSITE **Painstaking** paint job on this Evo, a fine example of the more abstract designs in favour in recent years

ABOVE, LEFT **More** elaborate engine work – modern heat-resistant paints are long lasting and look good. They've really taken over from engraving in engine decoration

BELOW, LEFT **Superb** airbrushed eagle head spruces up a front mudguard – plain pearl silver makes an effective background

OPPOSITE **The more you look at this design, the more you see**

ABOVE, RIGHT **These days, the engine often gets as much cosmetic attention as the rest of the bike. These RevTech heads have been coloured in heat-resistant paint, the barrels match the frame and tank and the tappet covers are chromed**

BELOW, RIGHT **The top end, money-no-object customs have both elaborate cosmetics and extensive tuning – Richard Taylor's twin supercharged machine is an example**

OPPOSITE **Nice update on the flame theme, which are now often reduced to stylised swirls – colours used on the tank and engine as well suggest this is a hot motor**

ABOVE, RIGHT **Consistency is quite satisfying in a paint job; some of the best examples carry the theme through to the mudguards and side panels, as on this Razorback**

BELOW, RIGHT **Colourful battery box on Tina Holtman's Razorback, which keeps the same wacky theme throughout**

RIGHT Gothic horror tank of the old school, which shows the same skill and attention to detail as later, more 'tasteful' works of tank art

painters are branching out too. One extension of the traditional fantasy art is the ethnic look – Native American or Celtic symbols are favourites (the latter in leatherwork as well) though more in patterns and designs than actual murals. Like the Gothics, this is backward-looking, and it's still true that few custom paint jobs use futuristic or sci-fi images. Animals are as popular as ever, usually of the legendary (Pegasus) or dangerous (birds of prey) variety. It has to be something denoting power and freedom – when did you last see a cute little grey squirrel airbrushed on the tank of a custom bike?

More recently, there have been bikes with ever more elaborate paint jobs – painstaking replicas of well known paintings, or Ty Lawer's airbrushed 50-dollar bills, so crumpled and used they look as if you could just peel them off the tank. Or there's the marble look. Hunter Simms chose this for his 1994 Harley, and painter Horst used a white/silver urethane paint from House of Kolor. In a quite separate trend from these intricate airbrushed works are the new breed of bold, simple graphic designs. These usually use a simple solid colour, such as bright yellow, for the background, overlaid with a graphic pattern in simple red or orange – the Wyatt bikes (see below) often used this. A variation is the 'splash' theme, often extended right over the whole bike from stem to stern. Giant drips of bright colour overlay the background shade, as if the bike has just ridden through a spray booth.

Sometimes engine details are picked out with the same base colour as well, to provide a key theme – the middle section of Harley-Davidson Evo cylinder heads is a good example – even the complete barrels may

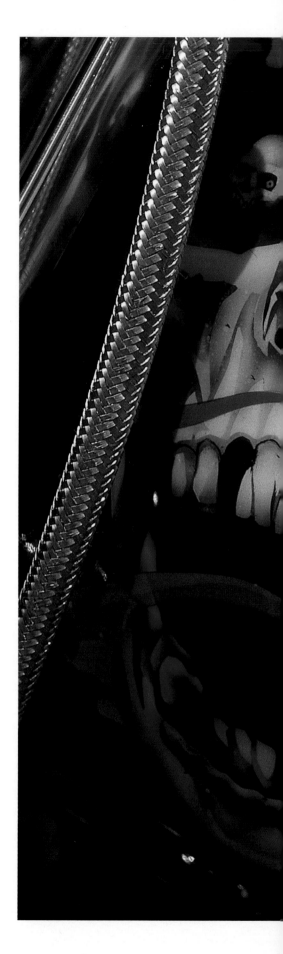

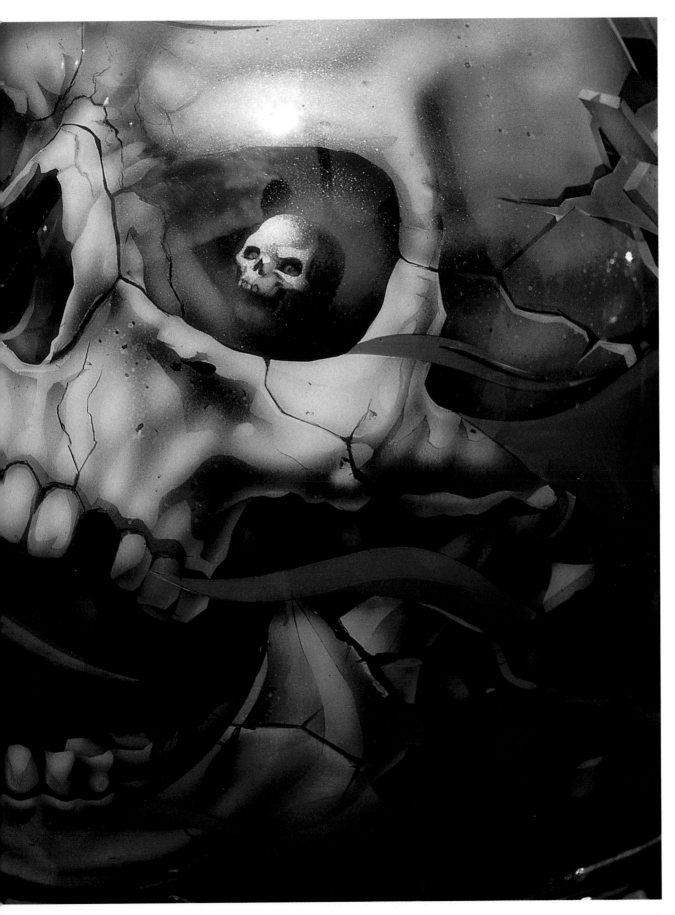

RIGHT **You can just see part of the seat mural on this bike of Mallard Teal's, which was stitched into the seat top**

OPPOSITE **Plain tank badge** shows that this bike hails from one of Harley's more sober periods. How the company decorated the machinery itself is an interesting reflection of contemporary culture through 90 years, from beautiful Art Deco designs to olive drab

ABOVE, LEFT **Primary belt drive** works well, but needs a vented cover to keep it cool – another opportunity for personalisation!

BELOW, LEFT **Speedo** is a certified Police one, while the paintwork is in something called Candy Brandywine

be painted. Anyway, the bold and simple approach to painting has a pleasing effect which makes the whole bike look clean and tidy. Interesting too that some of the mega-buck Harley customs now being built in the States are using very simple designs. If there is a 1990s trend in bike art, this is it. But the important point about paint is that painters, artists and builders now have the freedom to use whatever they like. That means more variety and new ideas, and a healthier custom bike movement.

ENGRAVING

Paint is as big a part of customizing as it ever was, but engraving seems to have passed its peak. It first appeared in the early '70s once metalflake paint became just too common. In a radical move (by the custom standards of the time) John Reed brought in an engraver from outside the business. His name was Don Bloxidge, a craftsman whose normal line of work

RIGHT Traditional red with yellow candy shadows, by Bob Gorske of Roade Studio. The rear shocks are aluminium items from Works Custom

LEFT The engine has been completely reworked with high compression pistons and Total Seal rings

OVERLEAF The last few bikes pictured have been based around older machines, but Tommy Jansson's was new in 1992. With more people prepared to spend a lot of money on customising, more bikes than ever are being personalised from new

ABOVE Engraving (on the timing cover) is more of a token offering here – the rest of the bike is a good example of less fussy 1990s work

RIGHT Rainbow Powder Coating did the business throughout this bike, which also has the almost obligatory six-pot brake callipers

involved engraving jewellery and gun barrels. Reed got him to apply the same swirly patterns to Old Don, his latest Triumph powered lowrider. Don obliged with his usual technique of complete freehand work, using just a hammer and chisel (albeit of a special kind).

It perhaps looks a little overdone now, with engraving on the timing and primary drive cover, the gearbox, pipes and rear wheel, but at the time it was new. And whatever you think of the design, you can't but wonder that the whole thing was done freehand. For a while, engraving was very popular, though never cheap. It allowed decoration of engine covers and other bits which couldn't be easily painted, and otherwise had to be plain chrome or polished aluminium. Although it still pops up here and there, engraving looks a bit too fussy to 1990s eyes, and you'd certainly never find it on one of the latest clean and simple bikes. But as with the paint, it's still around, lending variety and another point of interest.

TUNING

Speed was the whole reason customizing got started in the first place. But as the look became more crucial than mere miles per hour, the quest for speed took a back

seat. Neither did the classic chop itself lend itself to tuning – its whole persona was too laid-back for that, with a few exceptions. By and large, it's still true for most customizers; tuning is still an expensive business, and most would rather spend time and money on, say, raking the frame and having an airbrush paintjob, than on a super-light conrod that no-one will ever see. In any case, the latest Japanese and European superbikes, straight from the factory, are so mind-blowingly fast as to make any attempt to keep up either futile, or very, very expensive. But in the world of custom bikes, there are two exceptions to this, where making the bike go faster is still part of the whole appeal.

Streetfighters, which we touched on earlier, are the most obvious example. The whole look suggests power – tank, seat, headlight and instruments are often tiny items, just to emphasise the big, brutal engine and rear tyre. Japanese four cylinder engines are favoured, and not just because they have the required visual mass: they have more potential for power than any Harley. It's also interesting that builders often favour the old air-cooled engines over newer liquid-cooled ones. Not that they are any better as engines, but the finning makes them look more massive and 'mechanical' – the latest engines by contrast, look more like boring lumps of iron. A street fighter engine has to look

OPPOSITE **Engraving, in this case by Dave Perewitz of Cycle Fab, was sometimes taken to extremes, though this one is quite restrained. The bike is a low rider built by Mark Shadley**

ABOVE **So what does a professional customizer build for himself? Dave Perewitz's choice is this Shovelhead – no radical frame or wild engine, but the paint and engraving is all his own work**

RIGHT **Mallard Teal's** everyday road bike is this mildly modded FXE; it's a 1977 bike which Mallard has used as everyday transport since 1979

BELOW, RIGHT **The Teal FXE** does have a few modifications inside. The 80ci engine is standard size, but has polished ports and an Andrews 'A' cam. The gearbox uses Andrews parts too

powerful as well as be so. Not only that, but some of these bikes compete on the drag strips as well as being road legal. Of course, as with anything else, tuning is only limited by how much you want to spend. To the right is a typical example.

Bikes like that one are built to go fast – ten-second quarter mile times are not unusual on the drag strip. But there's another breed of serious tuner who has no intention of taking his/her bike into any sort of competition, unless it's for Best Paint. The bespoke custom builders in the States – Arlen Ness, Wyatt Fuller and the rest – will build a bike to your specifications. This all costs a great deal of money,

EUROPEAN STREETFIGHTER

Engine	Kawasaki four-cylinder DOHC, air-cooled
Power	154bhp (at rear wheel)
Capacity	1428cc
Cylinder head	Eight plug conversion, ported and flowed

Valves
  Inlet
  Exhaust
  Retainers
	
	39mm
	31mm
	Titanium

Cams
  Type
  Lift
	
	Kent Racing Pro Stock
	0.500in

Conrods	Standard, but polished and balanced
Crankshaft	Standard - polished, balanced and welded up

Carburettors
  Type
  Size
	
	Mikuni flatslides
	38mm

Ignition	Four 6v Dyna coils, with 9,000rpm rev limiter
Exhaust	Harris Formula 1
Clutch	Standard - Chevrolet springs
Frame	Standard Z1000 with RX1000 extended rear swinging-arm
Forks	Standard Z1000, home-made yokes
Brakes	Twin front discs (drilled) with Billet four-pot callipers

because the people involved want nothing but the best, and they can afford it. It's related to the eighties phenomenon of Hollywood bikers – however famous you were, the thing to be seen on was a Harley. Harleys are now highly fashionable with a well-heeled group of people who think nothing of $2,000 for a respray. They don't use their bikes every day, but they do want

the best of everything, and that includes the engine.

This isn't just the odd bit of gas-flowing. There's serious money involved, and the custom industry has been only too pleased to come up with four-valve heads and big-bore and stroker kits. Of course, people have always tuned Harleys; the conversion from 883 to 1200 is relatively simple and well worth doing. Before that, tuners tried all the usual things to make a relatively outdated powerplant keep up firstly with the

OVERLEAF **Richard Taylor**
masterminded this bike,
but emphasizes that many
were involved in its
execution, including
engineers Derek Chinn and
Dave Batchelor, with more
help from many others

British bikes, then the Japanese. And if you can't go to the expense of a two litre conversion, there are plenty of milder routes to more power. The standard air cleaner and box are usually junked in favour of a less restrictive one from S&S or perhaps Screamin' Eagle (the official Harley tuning parts label). On softly-tuned standard Harleys, the camshaft usually comes in for attention – an EV 141 Sifton is a common choice, though it needs adjustable pushrods as well. As for carburettors, some

RIGHT The engine is
mainly Harman – 120ci of
pure muscle, with twin
superchargers helping to
produce around 150bhp
on pump fuel, plus
tractor levels of torque.
Richard chose to stick
with two-valve heads,
rather than four-valve, but
fitted extra big poppets
to cope with the
supercharged air supply

favour the Mikuni smoothbore (in place of the standard Keihin) but for more top end power the S&S Super E is said to be the one to have. RevTech also sell a carb which comes with three sleeved sizes – 38, 42 and 45mm – the theory is that as the engine takes another step up the tuning ladder, you just pop a bigger sleeve in. It's also worth increasing the compression ratio to around 9.5:1, according to the experts, and using less restrictive pipes, such as Kerker or SuperTrapp.

That of course, is fairly mild tuning. This, on the other hand, is something else. Richard Taylor likes his projects to be out of the ordinary. "I like to be different, and the more difficult it is the better." With associate Dave Coomber he runs Bespoke/Taylor Made, based in the south-east of England. Most of what he does is custom Harleys (though at the time of writing he was also working on a Kawasaki ZZR1100 chop), and he decided to build a showcase bike. "Everything was done by hand. The bike had to start and run hot or cold. I wouldn't have built the bike just for show, so everything had to work, and work well. It was also built to demonstrate what I can achieve, plus what can be done in the UK."

Two years in the making ("a lot of lost sleep, headaches and too much money", adds Richard) the bike is an amazing amalgam of mostly handmade parts. The engine might look vaguely like a Harley V-twin, but there's very little that actually is. And the power output is very un-Harley like as well – Richard estimates a conservative 150bhp, and describes the torque as "tractor stuff". There's always the suspicion with this sort of bike that the only time it sees tarmac is from the back of a trailer, but Richard's bike is road legal. It does the odd

Harley Davidson...

short trip, but the bike's value puts a stop to everyday use. In any case, it certainly does the business at shows – Best in Show at the Kent Custom Show in 1995 and second at both Brighton and Genk.

The trouble is, a mere spec sheet can't do justice to this supercharged monster, because most of it is handmade. This is a new style of money-no-object customizing, built for riders who slap a blank cheque on the counter and don't care how many noughts it ends up with. Either that, or as a showcase for the company that built it – look, guys, this is what we can do. At this level, the philosophy is simple; there's no single part of the bike, however small, that can't be improved in some way; or better still, thrown away in favour of a hand crafted replacement. Richard Taylor's bike has hand-made fuel and oil tanks, though there's nothing very unusual about that. What sets it apart are all the little parts to suit the superchargers – the intake and exhaust manifolds, pressure relief valve, drive assembly and intake clamps. All made by hand from either alloy or stainless steel. Even the hubs, and details like cable clamps, chainguard and specialist bolts were all hand-made too. No wonder it took two years to build.

THE BUILDERS

There isn't room to mention here the hundreds of companies that build complete custom bikes from scratch. So with apologies to the many talented engine builders, artists and painters whose names don't appear, here are a few who represent different parts of the spectrum.

Mallard Teal's name comes up more than once in this book. Like Arlen Ness,

TAYLOR MADE

Engine	Harman pushrod V-twin, air cooled
Cylinder barrels	Harman
Capacity	120ci (1,953cc)
Cylinder heads	Harman
Valves	"Dinner plates"
Pistons	Aries, 4.75in
Camshafts	Andrews
Crankshaft	S & S
Conrods	Carillo
Superchargers	K.F. x 2
Carburettors Type Size	 Dellorto x 2 45mm
Air cleaner	K & N
Ignition	Hi-4
Exhaust Pipes Silencers	 Hand made, st. steel "Sort of"
Clutch	H-D wet multi-plate
Gearbox	H-D 5-speed
Brakes Front Twin discs, 4 x 6-pot Billet callipers Rear Single disc, 2 x 6-pot Billet callipers	
Suspension Front Suzuki GSXR 1100 forks, heavily modified. Handmade alloy yokes Rear H-D shocks, handmade stainless steel swinging arm	
Frame	P & D, c.1970, stretched with 35 degree rake

Mallard started out painting custom cars in the sixties. It was, oddly enough, the Vietnam War that put him on to bikes. With call-up papers in hand, Mallard realised that a car would just depreciate if he was away for a few years, but a Harley wouldn't, so he bought one. And in the

LEFT **Despite all the machinery, it's quite a slim bike, apart from the K.F. superchargers. "It was built to demonstrate what I can achieve, plus what can be done in the UK as well" – Richard Taylor. He's succeeded**

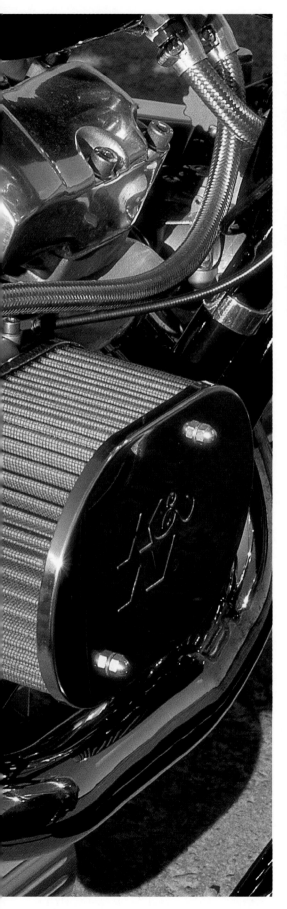

OPPOSITE **Hard to believe, not just that this bike is road legal, but that its owner actually uses it out in the traffic, despite its astronomical value (he describes the worth as similar to "a small house")**

LEFT **Matt Grimwall did the paintwork, an important factor in the bike's show successes in its first year – Best in Show at Kent, Best Press at Genk, among others**

twenty-odd years since then, he's concentrated on customizing them. He's one of those customizers who likes to do both paint and mechanical work, so the result can genuinely be called his own creation. Now, Mallard still builds Harleys for both himself and customers, from his workshop on Mounds Boulevard, St Paul, Minnesota.

Donnie Smith, another Minnesota man, started out about the same time. He was one of the names behind the SB&F custom shop, which was a respected part of the late 1960s scene. While brother Happy Smith and Bob Fetrow ran the workshop, Donnie looked after the retail side – the shop sold its own line of aftermarket parts as well as other people's. Despite this mainly administrative role, when the three partners went their separate ways in the mid-eighties, Donnie went on to build complete bikes, in a small way. Unlike Mallard Teal, Donnie's approach is to sub-contract work to specialists. Engine man Jim Ulasich for example, had done much of the engine work for SB&F. For his first solo project, Donnie comissioned Jim to convert a

OPPOSITE **Smooth flowing bodywork finishes off the rear end of Richard Taylor's showpiece, and uses the drip theme effectively**

ABOVE **Jim Randolph's Evo shows a number of different influences. the overall stance is lowrider, but it's also got some of the rangey look of a traditional chop. Paint by Mallard Teal**

LEFT **Ness side covers, Works shocks and Supertrapp exhaust. Jim Randolph's bike is a rolling exhibition for the custom parts makers**

PREVIOUS PAGE **Frame work was done by Donnie Smith** – stretched, lowered by two inches, and raked as well. Smith also supplied the swinging arm, and Mallard Teal painted the bike in Raspberry Metallic. B.T. did the graphics and striping

RIGHT **Painted heads and barrels to match the bike,** and the fins are polished. Air cleaner box is quite restrained

OPPOSITE **Chrome details on the engine** – note Arlen Ness 'A' timing cover, pushrod tubes and tappet covers

Shovelhead bottom end to accept an Evo top half, which itself was converted to a twin plug set-up. Likewise, Kevin Winter painted the bike, which went on to win acclaim for everyone involved.

ARLEN NESS

To call Arlen Ness an established part of the custom world is a bit of an understatement. Not only has he been in business for a very long time (setting up shop in the late 1960s), Arlen has succeeded by constantly coming up with new ideas. Not just selling familiar parts that people want to buy, but putting in his own ideas and so adding something to the custom movement.

He started out as a painter, doing such a great job on his first Harley Knucklehead that several people asked him to paint their bikes as well. Then he designed a new style of handlebar, the Ramhorn, his first successful accessory (Ness has always been about making and selling parts, as well as designing complete bikes). The little shop in his backyard was soon outgrown, so he

gave up the day job (Arlen was a removal man) and took the plunge. Since then, he hasn't looked back, and the Ness shop has become big business, with a massive catalogue of parts and large mail order sales, about 25% of them overseas.

What's particularly nice about the Ness story is that the whole family seem to be involved – his wife Bev and daughter Sherri work in the office, while Cory Ness acts as shop manager, as well as building the odd bike, just like his Dad.

Is there a Ness look? The simple answer is no, and that's probably one of the reasons for his continuing success. Although he is associated with Bay Area Lowriders, and low riding bikes have been a common Ness theme, you can't really point to any typically Ness features. He does like flames, but then so do thousands of other builders. He has built useable machines that could be ridden every day, but what everyone remembers are the wild show bikes, such as the twin-engined Two Bad and the outrageous Ferrari bike.

Take the Ferrari. It's really the ultimate bodywork bike, but completely different from those luxury liners. Everything screams performance (in a straight line, at least). The 265/60 rear tyre is wider than that of a genuine Ferrari Testarossa. The engine's flywheels are made by Harley, but very little else is; John Harmon supplied the barrels, heads and crankcases. With massive 4.25in pistons it gives 128ci displacement (that's nearly 2.1 litres). Each of these gargantuan cylinders is fed by its own Magnuson supercharger and two Dell'Orto carburettors. As if that wasn't enough, there are a couple of nitrous bottles as well. The aluminium bodywork (built by Craig Naff) is clearly Ferrari inspired, from the

RIGHT One of the few complete bikes built by Arlen Ness, based on a Springer Softail – Billet brake callipers are a common change

BELOW, RIGHT A rare one this. Wyatt Fuller built only twenty or so before H-D stepped in

Testarossa style intakes to the colour scheme (what else but red?) On the other hand, the FXR put together by Cory Ness for a Sturgis meet is quite the opposite. It's neat, clean and rideable, showing what can be done in a very short time (he had a month before leaving for the Black Hills) using off-the-shelf parts. A new front frame section stretched the bike, and raked WideGlide forks transformed the front end. The wheels started off solid, but were stylised by a CNC milling machine. The rest – mudguards, brake calipers, tuning parts – was over the counter.

The real answer to all this variety is that the Ness company comes up with something different every year. It's partly corporate promotion – cruising down Daytona's main street at the right time of year does more to raise the profile than any amount of advertising – but it's also clear that Arlen Ness designs these bikes because he enjoys it, and you can't have a better reason than that.

WYATT FULLER & RAZORBACK

Razorback is a relatively new name in customizing. Owner Wyatt Fuller set up shop in 1993, though he'd been building bikes part-time for a year or two before that. The day job was as a commercial pilot, but such is the burgeoning demand for bespoke custom Harleys (in the US at least) that Wyatt was able to throw it over and become a full-time builder of customs. His bikes catered for the top end of the market, where well-heeled owners come into the shop with a blank cheque (or at least a flexible budget) and some ideas.

It should all be past tense really, as about a year after Wyatt went full-time, Harley-Davidson bought him out. H-D, ever on the look out for someone with their finger on the custom pulse, hired Wyatt to have a hand in designing the Harley range of accessories. So there would be no more fully-built Razorback bikes, of which only about 20 were made before the takeover. This is a pity, because in the short time they were around, the Razorbacks did establish a style of their own.

Wyatt called it 'futuristic', not in a space age, sci-fi sort of way, but clean and solid, with nineties style graphics. Like the body-

RIGHT **Ken Denison's bike typifies the simple '90s look – one solid colour and some chrome, and that's it**

BELOW, RIGHT **Did you wonder why so many pictures in this book were taken from the righthand side? It's the side where those twin exhausts exit on a Harley. This is the 'dull' side of a Razorback. President Bill Clinton has been photographed in Milwaukee astride a standard Softail, as have, unsurprisingly, many politicians when they visit the city: perhaps this machine would have been more appropriate ...**

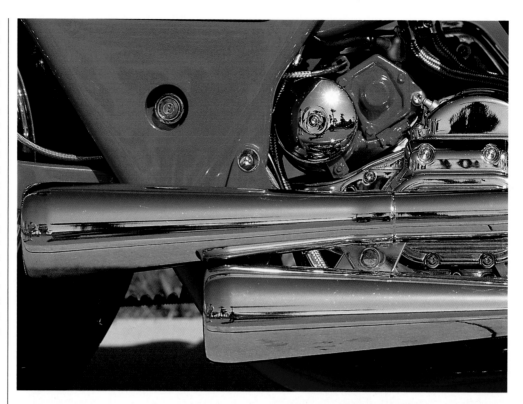

LEFT The money-no-object custom may have originated in the States, but Richard Taylor is aiming to build the same sort of ultimate bike for British and European customers

BELOW, LEFT Nice detail work on Nick Holmes' much modified FXR Harley, which was built by Battistinis of Bournemouth. The frame is virtually standard (no rake or stretch) but everything else is different. The fuel tank (stretched by 6") is a Battistini special, though many of the other parts are off-the-shelf – bars, grips and mudguards are all from Arlen Ness. Forks may look standard, but hide progressive springs and a detailing kit, while the wheels are more obviously special – Aero Spun Aluminium (made by PM) at both ends

RIGHT **Neat,**
unencumbered engine on
Tina Holtman's Razorback.
It is painted, but is still in
stark contrast to the bright
bodywork

BELOW, RIGHT **Sonny**
DePalma of Paint Mad Art
did the paintwork on Tina's
bike, a brash, bold
statement of colour

RIGHT **Rear wing is there**
to suggest a drag bike
look, though this
motorcycle is strictly for
the road only

LEFT **Soft pastel shades typify the Myer bike, which suggests its presence rather than shouts it**

BELOW, LEFT **Rectangular headlamps are rarely used now, though this one on Steve Myer's Razorback helps to emphasize the bulk of the beast**

On the image: World's Finest Products For Harley-Davidsons — Tour de Chrome '94

work bikes, there was a tendency towards making the bikes look solid and substantial, with nothing sprouting or spindly. But they didn't have all-enveloping bodywork. While the mudguards were large and valanced, the wheels were still on show, and the engine definitely was – Razorbacks were always naked bikes, without a fairing in sight. The attention to detail showed up in the efforts to hide away all possible pipes and wires, especially up in the handlebar area, and the smoothed-out contours of the frame joints and bodywork. Some customers still wanted turn signals, but standard flashers would have stuck out in crude contrast to the overall harmony. So a Razorback favourite was tiny lights (one inch square at most) which clung discreetly to the sides of the bike.

What Wyatt didn't do was serious frame modifications: in silhouette, the Razorbacks look remarkably standard, but it's the details that count. If owners didn't want straight graphics, the familiar Harley eagle was a recurring theme, but rarely as a straight portrait. More often it would be

part bird, part Boeing 747, or (as on Dan Sargeant's Fat Boy) a mechanised mix of well-oiled parts. The actual paintwork and design was farmed out; Dawn Holmes of Air Craft and Sonny DePalmera of Paint Mad Art were the regulars. Many of the bikes sported Fat Boy disc wheels with holes or slots machined into them. This became a lucrative business in itself, with customers sending their wheels in to be worked on. The resulting look was really an extension of the billet philosophy – the wheels looked as if they'd been carved from solid.

The Wyatt Razorbacks were bikes of their time, built for rich customers who knew what they wanted and could pay someone else to do it. In the 1990s, custom bikes in general, and Harleys in particular, are fashionable. But the backbone of the movement hasn't changed. Across the world, thousands of riders are personalising their bikes in their own way. Whatever style they choose, whatever paint job or engine, it's all down to the individual. And that's why the custom scene is thriving.